10 KEY BUSINESS OUTSOURCING INGREDIENTS

FREE UP YOUR ADMIN AND SALES TEAMS

10 KEY BUSINESS OUTSOURCING INGREDIENTS

FREE UP YOUR ADMIN AND SALES TEAMS

by Marisa Wiman

Business Freedom Lifestyle

 2014

Copyright © 2014 by Marisa Wiman

All rights reserved. This book or any portion thereof may not be reproduced or used in any manner whatsoever without the express written permission of the publisher except for the use of brief quotations in a book review or scholarly journal.

Fourth Revision: 2014

ISBN 978-1-291-76878-7

Business Freedom Lifestyle
Focal Point 2nd Floor

18 Second Avenue
COTTON TREE, Queensland, Australia, 4558

www.businessfreedomlifestyle.com

Ordering Information:
Special discounts are available on quantity purchases by corporations, associations, educators, and others. For details, contact the publisher at the above listed address.

U.S. trade bookstores and wholesalers: Please contact Business Freedom Lifestyle Tel: +61(0) 7 3503 6835
Fax: +61(0) 7 5492 8822 or
email sales@businessfreedomlifestyle.com

Business Freedom Lifestyle

The trademarks used in this book are owned by BFL Limited licensed for use by Business Freedom Lifestyle.
Greymouse trademark printed with permission.
Merendi, and Sunshine Coast Pet Resort logos are printed with permission.

Greymouse

Dedication

To my loving husband, team and friends
that stood by my life's journey.
Thank you. Without your support and
teaching me patience I would not have achieved
my dream lifestyle.

Contents

Acknowledgements ix

Preface xi

Introduction 1

Chapter 1: Outsource What? 3

Chapter 2: Virtual Training 9

Chapter 3: Building Trust 15

Chapter 4: Countries Culture 21

Chapter 5: Language Barriers 27

Chapter 6: Virtual vs. Physical 31

Chapter 7: Full or Part Time 37

Chapter 8: Results 41

Chapter 9: Document Systems 45

Chapter 10: Manage Remotely 49

Appendix 1 - Questions 55

Appendix 2 - About the Author 63

Appendix 3 – Tours, Sharing Ideas ... 65

Appendix 4 - Learn More 67

Appendix 5 – Supporter 75

Acknowledgements

I like to acknowledge the Fiji and Philippine teams. We were all pioneers when we started, and I am proud to say we still have a few team members whom joined us and shared our vision. Thank you for believing in my vision!

Also a special acknowledgement must go to all of our 'early adopters' that became customers. Together we refined the services, made mistakes, improved and continued. Many of these customers are still with us today and achieved massive freedom and cash flow to grow other businesses, sell their business or in some cases semi retire.

I cannot forget to acknowledge the 'visionary mindset' of my husband Kelvin. Without him and his ever bright view of the future, I would not have written this book.

Preface

Outsourcing, Virtual Assistants, Personal Assistants, and Virtual Workforce such a commonly used words now! However it was not that way in 2002, while I was sitting in an office in Suva (Fiji Islands in the South Pacific) and the idea of delivering services to the world via the internet came to mind.

Everyone in Australia was getting well familiar with the 'after hours calls' received by some distant Indian call centre. The thought of having someone from another county working closely with you was still 'green'. In fact my idea was rejected by the majority of the people I spoke to at the time. I had to wait two years before being able to surround myself with a technically minded and capable team to implement the technology to create a Virtual Workforce. The idea was born!

Taking the idea, the concept of helping as many people as I could grew to become a living story of what I did to free up my personal time and subsequently every business I've touched since then.

I am very passionate about freedom and cashflow in my life and sharing the process I used. I am also very impatient and I had to learn how to handle this part of my personality.

Over the years I become known as the SME (Small and Medium Enterprises) Virtual Workforce Queen. This book's lessons and stories come from real life, based on the experience of living each step myself. I have also shared some experiences guiding and observing some of our client's growth.

My other passion is helping people. Probably because I lived in Fiji for a few years I saw the need to give our 'next door neighbours' an opportunity to use their skills, University degrees and passion for work in return of a wage that feed families and pay for educating the families. Many third world countries do not have social security, so this Virtual Workforce idea continues to make a difference in many people's lives.

Marisa Wiman

Introduction

Years ago, cost or headcount reduction were the most common reasons to outsource. Today the drivers are often more strategic, and focus on carrying out core value-adding activities in-house where an organisation can best utilise its own core competencies.

Why Outsource?

- Reduce operating costs
- Improve company focus
- Gain access to world class talents
- Extend working hours up to 24x7x365
- Insufficient resources available in the organisation
- Share risks with a partner company

Outsourcing activities have grown immensely over the years, and outsourcing has proven to have a substantial impact within organisations.

For larger businesses, It involves transferring of an inter-organisational business function or functions to an external service provider who agrees to perform the task for a specific time period, at an agreed upon price.

The decision to outsource is an easy one but the way it is to be handled and the strategic decisions that need to be taken form the key to successful outsourcing.

 Hot Tips are placed within this book to describe critical points or money and time saving ideas.

Chapter 1: Outsource What?

Your email in-box is full but you have no time to go through it, let alone respond. You have a zillion calls to be returned and a bunch of paper work to be signed. Helppp!

Fortunately for you, help is right around the corner. Email, phone calls, sales processes, and marketing research would be the most common tasks that can be outsourced.

According to a research company in the United States, the average number of email messages we get per day is 110 and we send 35. Depending on the business you are in, you will receive important calls that must be addressed the same day or you might lose business.

Routine jobs like management of your email in-box, responding and returning calls can be outsourced. In my experience, these are areas where you can get help from someone who will take the entire responsibility of ensuring you do not miss out on any important sales or customer interaction.

10 Key Business Outsourcing Ingredients

Here are five routine but important tasks that can be outsourced:
- All your phone calls - in bound and out bound
- All your incoming emails
- Your websites updates
- Your sales processes
- Your customer service follow up

A customer example follows to give you a practical idea of the outcomes.

Example - Sunshine Coast Pet Resort

Building a small business can be challenging and stressful. When Sam Brown of the Sunshine Coast Pet Resort began to investigate ways to grow her business on a tight budget,

Marisa Wiman

never in a million years did she think that an offshore Call Centre could fit her business model.

After several years of being challenged by the level of service provided by her Pet Resort (particularly having customers not being able to 'get through'), Sam took a leap of faith that freed her from the 'day to day' challenge of managing the phones, to being in a place where valuable resources were re-directed to pet-care activities and being in the enviable position where she saved over 40% per year in customer service costs. So what were her challenges?

"The Pet Resort is a small business, how could it warrant using a Call Centre? Aren't they reserved for BIG organisations?

Sam's Pet Resort had grown in 10 years from an annual turnover of $100,000 to $800,000. At her lowest point, her wages (including paying herself) soared to 49% of turnover and it became really difficult to make a profit. A transformation of her business practices (including creating a fully documented Quality System) meant that in an 18-month period, the wages were around 41% of turnover. But after realising that she and her partners had invested around 3 million dollars, and were struggling to get an appropriate return, it was time to really look "outside the square."

10 Key Business Outsourcing Ingredients

In February 2008, Sam was presented with a huge challenge. Her Customer Service Manager and Office Junior walked off the job due to a difference of 'opinion regarding acceptable behaviour standards.'

Left high and dry, Sam turned this obstacle into an opportunity by seeking better ways of functioning. Jo Hassan, her business partner, came across a Brisbane firm called Greymouse who were offering Call Centre services to small businesses. The owners of Greymouse were also customers of the Pet Resort, so they really understood the 'sensitive' nature of the business (that is, you are looking after people's babies). A proposal was forwarded by Greymouse, which stated that all phone calls would be answered within the first 3 rings, at a cost equivalent to 40% LESS than the pay of an Office Junior.

This meant that the resources for the Customer Service position could now be redistributed to direct pet care.

The end financial result was a total wages bill of 32% of turnover.

Pet Resort witnessed amazing results! Greymouse provided a viable business option for a small business to utilise a 'state-of-the-art' Call Centre. Although, the Pet Resort had previously invested in a PABX and other telephony infrastructure, it was still worth making the

Marisa Wiman
move. The company benefited from the available resources and expertise offered by Greymouse. Working with Greymouse is like having your very own in-house IT Department.

Outsourcing' is like shopping on line. You purchase a few things from an online store, you test them out and if you find them of good quality, you keep buying more from them.

10 Key Business Outsourcing Ingredients

Let's do it

Ask yourself these questions,

List what I hate doing in the office
How many calls do I miss (or miss completing) each day?
How many hours do I work each day / week?

Chapter 2: Virtual Training

Knowing how to train a virtual employee will save you time, money and stress.

You wish to grow your business and you have decided to take on extra hands on board. Smart thinking!

But now, time to find an organisation that can supply you with capable resources that fit your business model. Once you zero in on one and finalize the deal, you will then have to start training them. The future of your outsourcing depends on this training.

The 3 training methods that can be used:
- You travel to the country where the employee is
- You use Skype or Lync to deliver the training course
- You fly the employee to your office

Whatever method you choose, it is imperative that you have a clear understanding of your specific outsourcing need before making that all important final decision.

10 Key Business Outsourcing Ingredients

Even if you have decided to take the virtual long-distance route, the training must be handled as you would if the person was with you. You should keep the documentation ready well in advance, and you just share the info electronically instead of paper-based communication.

The 3 possible mistakes when training a virtual employee
- Assuming that the person you employed already knows who you are and what you do
- Forgetting to test their knowledge retention skills
- Giving too many tasks at once

Example – Beautician

Sally is a beautician in Perth. She wanted to get away to Bali for a couple of weeks; she did not want to miss out on business while she was away enjoying herself. She engaged the services of Greymouse and trained a Virtual Receptionist to take calls in her absence and to make bookings so that she returned to an overflowing appointment book.

Marisa Wiman

In her own words: "it just worked!" "I trained Navina to log into my Google Calendar, explained to her how my business works and the services I delivered, and Navina took the task very seriously, and definitely booked me in for 2 weeks full time while I was away! Loved it and I'm now planning my holiday next year. Thank you."

'Training a virtual employee' is like training an in-house employee, but without the need for the employee's physical presence.

"If you're trying to achieve, there will be roadblocks. I've had them; everybody has had them. But obstacles don't have to stop you. If you run into a wall, don't turn around and give up. Figure out how to climb it, go through it, or work around it".

Michael Jordan

10 Key Business Outsourcing Ingredients

Marisa Wiman

Let's do it

Ask yourself these questions

Do I need a holiday? When and where?
Write down a few things that could be done without me 1. 2.
How do I feel about the idea of Virtual Resources working with me?

10 Key Business Outsourcing Ingredients

Chapter 3: Building Trust

Knowing how to build trust will help you grow your business faster.

The company you decide to work with must have enough supporting information to confirm that they have been in business for at least five years. You must be provided with a list of current clients they work with and references should be clearly visible on their business websites.

The key to successful outsourcing is trust. Trust is not something that can be bought. It is built! Trust keeps the world together, whether it is business relationships or personal. We have all seen how some employees have a high degree of trust in their leaders and it shows in their commitment that in turn leads to higher productivity.

Start off small and as your confidence grows in your outsourcing company, gradually increase the services you would like to outsource.

The 7 questions on how to build trust
- How did you hear about the outsourcer?
- Have you interviewed them?
- Have you checked out their references?
- Have you met the owners of the business (even if it's on Skype)

10 Key Business Outsourcing Ingredients

- Have you checked out their profiles on social networking sites like Linkedin, FB etc?
- Have you spoken to their employees?
- What is your gut feeling about the company

Example – Markinson Brisbane, Australia

CEO of Markinson in Brisbane using Outsourcing Services 24x7x365

What was the main reason you selected Greymouse?

In choosing a call centre provider, Markinson was looking for an organisation that not only had the necessary experience but also one which closely aligned with Markinson's ethos of being a customer focused, people inspired organisation. Upon investigation and discussions with Greymouse, we felt very comfortable that these needs would be met.

What benefit have you received?

By far the biggest benefit we have received is peace of mind - knowing that regardless of the nature or the timing of the call, our customers

Marisa Wiman
would receive top quality first level customer interaction by friendly staff

'Placing your trust' in an organisation that supplies virtual resources is like a mum leaving her child in a childcare centre and hoping/expecting that her baby is taken care of at all times. When you outsource, you must trust and have the confidence that your clients are taken care of in the same way.

Trust must be built, earned and then cultivated. It is not given and once you get it, treasure it.

10 Key Business Outsourcing Ingredients

> *"None of us knows what might happen even the next minute, yet still we go forward. Because we trust. Because we have Faith."*
> *Paulo Coelho*

Let's do it

Ask yourself these questions

Did I contact a Virtual Resources provider today?
Did I check the references and speak to their employees? What did I find?
Do I know enough to trust them?

10 Key Business Outsourcing Ingredients

Marisa Wiman
Chapter 4: Countries Culture

Different countries have different cultures. The sooner you understand them, the quicker you can embrace the virtual workforce you engage.

We use Fiji and Philippines as the two countries of choice. Fiji is a country where service is considered king! People are friendly, patient, and their English has a nice accent. Philippines have many hard workers suitable for back office functions. The Philippine American accent is sometimes rejected by businesses, however accepted when they expand products or services to overseas to locations like America. Matching the outsourcing countries culture and accent with your business needs is fundamental for your success.

An example of cultures includes differences in public holidays. Fiji includes 8 gazetted public holidays per year, Australia has about 8 (depending on the state) and Philippines reaches 21 gazetted public holidays each year. Philippines also have thirteen (13) monthly pays each year. *(This number is not a mistake)*. Planning your business outsourcing needs includes the delivery data and how you will manage different countries public holidays.

10 Key Business Outsourcing Ingredients

For office work and administration type work, you need to have friendly and patient people. If you need other services, such as website developers or designers, you would look toward bigger countries such as Philippines, India or China.

Based on my experience, you must make sure that the company you deal with has a very solid Company Policy based on trust, honesty and integrity. They must also have a binding employment agreement and non-disclosure agreement.

The 3 keys to bridge the gap between cultures
- Engage with the culture that matches yours the most
- Understand what makes the virtual employees give their best
- Visit the country and your virtual team on the pretext of a holiday

Example - Michelle from Balloonaversal in Melbourne , Australia:

Creating a position that required "no workers compensation" and "no annual leave" but

Marisa Wiman

still have a full-time person - seemed like an impossible dream.

We already had an online CRM (Customer Relations Management) in place which handles all of our quotes, invoices, and purchase orders tracking the sales. It also includes client files, booking Calender, and artists/performers. These days it is called a "Cloud CRM," so I believe we were considered as "technology early adopters."

Then we decided to search online for a resolution to our problem and found Greymouse. The owners are Marisa and Kelvin who reside on the Sunshine Coast in Queensland, but have their back office team in Fiji. We approached them with our dilemma, and they helped us create our "impossible dream."

We recruited Alisi (an employee of Greymouse), whom we really adore as she does such a great job for us. She has really stepped up to the plate and closes sales better than ever (even better than me). Alisi works 40 hours per week (Mon –Fri, 9am-5.30pm) around $500 per week giving us a HUGE saving of 50%.

10 Key Business Outsourcing Ingredients

 'Understanding the culture of the country you outsource to' is akin to visiting an airport. Until you land and go through the 'arrival doors' you do not know how they will welcome you. With guns or playing guitars!

> *Until you talk to a person, you do not know anything about him/her. You ask the first question and the rest will follow. – Anonymous*

Let's do it

Ask yourself these questions

Have I researched the Virtual Resources country?
Am I concerned? (Examples) - Accent? - Time zones? - Potential Barriers?
Have I skyped the future Virtual Resource?

10 Key Business Outsourcing Ingredients

Marisa Wiman
Chapter 5: Language Barriers

A universal language for communication: this is what you would wish for when outsourcing; however knowing how to overcome the language barriers will put you ahead of the competition.

Interview the person you are going to engage. Have a friendly chat with her/him and identify if you are going to like each other. Test the person for a few days to make sure she/he understands your business. Make them feel at ease by sharing some of your funny stories and explain how you operate, and let them know your likes and dislikes.

Have Skype chats, Lync conversations and phone calls to make sure there is a match. Once you find that perfect match, accents and other imperfections in language will fade into the background. Since the employee develops an understanding of your business, products, services and your style of functioning, they will easily be able to fit in with your organisation.

The 3 questions on overcoming the language barrier

- Do you have different ways of saying a specific word? Ie. Beeper or pager?

10 Key Business Outsourcing Ingredients

- Do you use Sir/Madam or call people by their Christian names?
- Do you use an Australian or American diary?

Example – Baloonaversal (Continued)

"Initially Alisi required a lot of training in the Balloonaversal business to understand what activities and services we provide.

Face painting, pony rides, balloon twisting for parties and corporate clients, travel times, suppliers, web sites, and CRM training went on for some time.

An example is Alisi's ability to communicate with our artist and performers through text messages from her PC in a two way conversation. This allows appointments, changes to be sent (SMS) almost instantly."

'Overcoming a language barrier' is like driving through a foggy road. Slow down and go through it as there is clear vision on the other side of the fog.

Marisa Wiman

Problems do not go away. They must be worked through or else they remain, forever a barrier to the growth and development of the spirit. – M Scott Peck

10 Key Business Outsourcing Ingredients

Let's do it

Ask yourself these questions

Am I concerned about the language differences?
Am I ready to spend 1 hour a day to teach my Virtual Resource?
What is going through my mind?

Marisa Wiman
Chapter 6: Virtual vs. Physical

Keep it simple and think of the advantages. For one thing, you do not have to make coffee for your virtual team! Oh! But you may be missing out on them making coffee for you, then that's a small price to pay!

The HR department in your organisation might get a bit worried about HOW to induct the new virtual employee.

Do not get all flustered!

Start discussing with your new employee on Skype. Share your organisation's internal documentation and soon you will find the ice breaking, It will not be long before they get used to your company and your way of working.

The HR management of the virtual employee is handled by the outsourced organisation, so you get to enjoy the services of the employee in your business, but without the hassles of managing the actual resource.

I encourage you to invite your virtual team member to your weekly meetings along with your physical team members.

If you have products like t-shirts or mugs or any other gadgets branded to your company, I suggest you send them over to your virtual team. They will love it and it will make them feel more a part of your team.

10 Key Business Outsourcing Ingredients

Take sufficient care of the new relationship as it is no different than any other business relationship. Never adopt an "out of sight, out of mind" approach.

The 5 reasons for preferring a virtual employee over a physical employee
- No Superannuation, leave loading or HR management
- No requirement for office space
- No penalty for working weekends, public holidays or after hours (in most outsourced countries)
- You can work in your PJs even if you are surrounded by virtual employees (they do not get to see you)
- Massive cost savings

Example - Teleconferencing Business

Clinton used to be woken up every night by clients calling him to ask 'how to use his conference system.' His local employee did not want to be woken up, unless he was getting paid for. The business did not have enough cash to pay for the extra after hour cost, so Clinton (being the owner) took this task on board.

Marisa Wiman

One day he contacted us asking for assistance that was within his budget. This was 4 years ago. We allocated 24x7x365 resources to take all of his calls and help where needed.

His business tripled in the last 3 years and all without Clinton having to spend extra money on wages. The service delivered is constant and a working system is now in place to cater for the next stage of business growth.

'Virtual versus physical employee' is like playing at casinos online where you don't have to dress up in formal clothing or offer tips to the dealers, but you get to enjoy all the casino games of your choice.

> *I like to connect to people in the virtual world, exchanging thoughts and ideas, when in the physical world we might never have the opportunity to cross paths. – Demi Moore*

10 Key Business Outsourcing Ingredients

Let's do it

Ask yourself these questions

Can I see myself NOT doing these tasks
How much I am saving by using the Virtual resource?
How do I present the idea to the rest of the team?

10 Key Business Outsourcing Ingredients

Chapter 7: Full or Part Time

An in-depth understanding of your business needs and performing the necessary due diligence work before outsourcing; will make it easier for you to identify the type of resource that suits you. It will also help you figure out the number of hours in a day you will be engaging their services.

Your Personal Assistant or Receptionist can be engaged for as long or as short a while, based on your requirement. For those of you that are unsure, my suggestion has always been to start off small and then increase the number of hours as you go.

Maintain a clear and strong communication channel with the Outsourcing organisation to make sure you are not locked into any strict contract, enabling you to expand or shrink as needed.

Eventually, if you get busier, you will need to move towards a fully dedicated resource to meet the increasing demands of your organisation.

The 3 elements of full time versus part time employee

Knowing that you can expand or shrink your virtual resources gives you massive power to:

- Not worry about office space
- Delegate more work, leaving you more time to handle your business
- Take on more business with the confidence that you have a strong support system in place

Example of a flexible virtual resource provider

"When things were a bit tight for us financially during the early part of 2010, Marisa happily put our hours to half time for a few months. (Our really quiet months)."

A 'Full-time' position is like eating three lavish meals. 'Part-time' is to skip dinner as two meals a day are enough!

Marisa Wiman

> *Friendship is a pretty full-time occupation if you really are friendly with somebody. You can't have too many friends because then you're just not really friends. – Truman Capote*

10 Key Business Outsourcing Ingredients

Let's do it
Ask yourself these questions

Do I need a part time or full time resource and why?
When do I need help the most?
Am I ready for it?

Chapter 8: Results

Measure to manage and you cannot go wrong! What you measure will grow.

Remember that generally team members do what is Inspected NOT what is expected!

If you have a CRM (Customer Relationship Management) system, you will be able to extract statistics to measure the productivity of your virtual team member.

If you do not have a CRM, your team member can keep a manual report of his/her activity. The key is to measure what is done (ie. how many calls made or received, how many emails handled, tickets logged, appointments made, etc.). These reports can be submitted for your perusal weekly, bi-monthly or monthly.

The 5 reasons for meeting expectations and measure results

- You can quickly identify if the virtual employee is doing his/her job
- Monitor deliverables and deadlines with your clients
- Take on new business based on the delivery times
- Nothing slips through the cracks
- You are in control of your business as you know what everyone is up to

10 Key Business Outsourcing Ingredients

Example – Measurement

Sam and Jo from the Pet Resort get a weekly report on every transaction and contact point the virtual team does for them. The report contains data and diagrams to show the actual situation of the bookings, sales and enquiries. Currently, the virtual team handles more than 3000 contact points a month (meaning emails, phone calls, text messages, and web chats).

'Meeting expectations and measuring the results' is like losing weight. You maintain a record of everything you eat as well as your activity each day, for the sake of accountability. The results will show at the end of the week.

Marisa Wiman

> *The man who cannot endure to have his errors and shortcomings brought to the surface and made known, but tries to hide them, is unfit to walk the highway of truth.- James Allen*

10 Key Business Outsourcing Ingredients

Let's do it
Answer these questions

What reports do I need to see?
What access do I need to give to the Virtual Resource?
What training I need to give?

Chapter 9: Document Systems

The quicker you document the process, the better it is for outsourcing the task.

Do not panic if you do not have a system in place. If you have it in your head, you can 'dump' it down and leave it to your Virtual Assistant to put it into a proper document. An easy task once you start with the process!

If you are a paper-based business, the data can be transferred into an excel document or into your CRM. Systems will help you grow your business in a 'controlled' manner. Creating a written system can take time and effort, but it is VITAL for the future of your business. You may decide on a single system or multiple, based on the nature of your business.

The 5 most important points in documenting a system
- Write it down
- Use screen capture to show various screens or examples (a picture is worth a thousand words)
- Keep it simple so that multiple people can follow it
- Start from the most basic tasks and proceed to the complicated ones

10 Key Business Outsourcing Ingredients

- Do not give up, just keep doing it a bit at the time

Example – Web site designer and marketing specialist

James just started with a part-time Virtual Assistant. Grace spent a week with James understanding the business and how James operates. James passed on his knowledge to Grace, and Grace prepared a written manual with the key information to allow herself and others to perform the task required by James.

The manual created by Grace has pictures, log-in information, and key information to make life easier when the task is being done.

'Documenting the system' is like a cook writing down step-by-step recipe of an apple pie so that it turns out perfect!

Think it, dump it and implement it! – Marisa Wiman

Marisa Wiman

10 Key Business Outsourcing Ingredients

Let's do it

Answer these questions

Do I have all the systems written down?
Do I check calls made or received (do a QA?)
Am I using the Virtual Resource to help me document what is in my head?

Marisa Wiman
Chapter 10: Manage Remotely

By discussing your needs with the outsourcing organisation, you can come up with several ways of monitoring your virtual team.

One of the common practices today is to install cameras where your virtual works. I find this option quite interesting as you can keep an 'eye' on your virtual team. But it is up to your outsourcing company to offer you this option. You might not use it all the time; however when you wish to call them, it would be nice to know that they are at their desk and able to talk to you.

If this is not an option with your outsourcing organisation, you manage them by way of reporting or by communicating on Skype, Lync or email.

Be prepared to share and learn from the outsourcing company you are working with. An open mind will allow you to quickly embrace the proven systems they have in place and adapt them to your business.

10 Key Business Outsourcing Ingredients

The 5 Most Important Virtues of Managing Remote Resources
- Enjoying the relationship
- Patience and consistency in training
- Listening to what your virtual team is asking
- Helping as much as you can in creating the documentation needed, enabling them to deliver a top-notch service
- Having the confidence that it will work and that you will gain the time and freedom to work on growing the business

The outsourcing process becomes easy when the client has a manual that can be followed. The virtual team member reads the manual, logs into the system, tries out what is in the manual and the owner of the business coaches where needed.

Example – Client Feedback

"We needed someone who would use our systems manual, follow the sales procedure, organise the parties and corporate events, and respond to customers' questions using our

Marisa Wiman

standard answer sheets. They need to be familiar with the internet, professional when answering the phone, responding to e-mails, able to use SMS and can assist our customers. While it sounds simple, it requires focus dedication and above all accuracy.

Managing remote resources is like managing a household full of teenagers.

Iphone, FB, Skype, Viber and other apps allow both parties to have a better communication. Use the tools given and available to make sure the end result is achieved for your business. Be flexible and have respect for each other. The tasks will get done and your stress level will reduce.

Be firm but fair and care for your remote resources as much as you would care for your teenager. Oh also remember to have fun with them and at the same time to keep an eye on them!

Check their work, give them feedback, use tools such as 'Time Doctor' to make sure the jobs are getting done and remember to celebrate victories together. After all you all work as a 'team' regardless of the location you are working from.

10 Key Business Outsourcing Ingredients

 The sense of vision, observation, togetherness, informality, collaboration and trust is achieved by using electronic means such as teleconferences, regular meetings, personal visits at least once a year. In today's business environment, a high level of open communication is required to keep the balance.

> *Work is a thing you do, not a place you go* – Simon Le Compte

Let's do it

Ask yourself these questions

Have I spoken to my Virtual Resource?
Am I building a rapport with him/her?
Did I share the company vision?

10 Key Business Outsourcing Ingredients

Thank you for making the time in your day to read this book. What I wrote is simple and based on experience.

I had to learn these steps myself first, before I could assist our clients and team members in how to work together.

I wish you freedom and a wonderful lifestyle in your business.

Appendix 1 - Questions

The most common area of concern is in reference to voice systems and quality.

How do voice systems work?

The voice quality must be perfect. Skype ® is acceptable for computer to computer, however it is not suitable for a business grade reception service. Reason include,
- Accumulative cost
- The time delay between ringing and answering,
- Distortions on the line

A business grade service will have a voice system as part of the support agreement.

The setup steps are simple;

1. You are provided a phone number as close as possible to your local area. This is a VoIP number that takes the inbound call
2. You then redirect your 1300 number or your phone to your new VoIP number.
3. The provider will set up the systems for you with the queues, messages, ringing

10 Key Business Outsourcing Ingredients

       and capability to have your receptionist answer, then action the call.
4. The receptionist should be able to take messages, send email or SMS, then transfer urgent calls directly to your mobile or landline. If you are waiting on that important call, you need it to be sent to you anywhere 24/7.

Call Quality & Resiliency

Quality of the call and time delay when speaking and listening is critical to having a good conversation. Suggestions;

1. Test and compare time delays
2. Ask if the provider has a backup Voice system, in case of internet outages or equipment failure
3. Ask about a second site (resiliency) and how long before this is active to take calls. You do not want to risk outages from Typhoons, Hurricanes or Cyclones.

Marisa Wiman

Common questions and answers provided daily.

What are the differences between a VR, VA, PA?

VR- Virtual Receptionist takes calls and transfer or delivers messages. This is a simple way to enter and try the services.

VA – Virtual Assistant handles sales processing of orders, collection of client details or client support role. They call customers back and complete surveys, or

PA – A Personal Assistant is dedicated to the business owner and business. They often make flight bookings, accommodation, and email responses on your behalf. A high degree of trust is required before you reach this level of service.

10 Key Business Outsourcing Ingredients

How do I specify greetings & scripts?

Provide your Virtual Receptionists with the greeting scripts of your choice as well as instructions for answering incoming customer calls. That way you will ensure that your calls are answered as your business and your company name. Most important is to maintain your business culture.

How do I divert my phone

The partner that you use will provide you with a dedicated local phone number. Simply forward your existing phone number (local or Toll Free 1300) to the number allocated to you. If you have a 'local' number all diverted phone calls are low cost.

Can I divert my mobile?

Yes you can. In an iPhone ® it is in 'Settings>Phone>Call Forwarding'. Switch it on, then enter your receptionist number.

Marisa Wiman

Start Taking Calls 24 /7?

Expanding your availability for your clients up to 24 hours per day gives you a competitive advantage in the market. Some providers do not offer this extended hours service, check that they do have this service before you start.

Can you start straight away?

Providers will have receptionists trained and on standby ready to start taking your calls. Test them and ensure they answer calls within three rings maximum.

The call answering is simple

1. Your customer calls
2. The call is directed to the Voip number
3. Calls are answered by friendly receptionists.
4. If you are available, virtual receptionists instantly transfer important calls directly to your phone (landline or mobile).
5. If you are unavailable, the receptionist advises that you are busy and then proceeds to action the request.

10 Key Business Outsourcing Ingredients

Is it easy to physically meet the virtual team?

Yes Fiji at 3.5 hours flying, is easier to reach than the Philippines with 10 – 12 hours travel time. Merendi recently visited the office in Fiji, sharing her experience with me. The family then had a holiday while they visited Fiji.

I recently had the pleasure of visiting Fiji to meet Shobna and her team of VRs & VAs and to train my new VA Binita. They were most welcoming when we arrived and made my partner and I feel very much at home. Prior to arriving in Suva Shobna was very helpful in providing information on accommodation where we could stay and she also organized a taxi to pick us up from the airport to our resort. The team at Greymouse were friendly and were very open to having us visit and work with them for the day. Shobna and her team are always helpful and there is nothing they won't do for you. Their goal is to ensure their clients' needs are met and of course they always exceed this.

merendi

Marisa Wiman

Is the business trip tax deductible?

If you already have a business relationship with your virtual team members, and your travel is for the purpose of meeting the team and spending time with them teaching, training or learning what is possible in the virtual world, by definition it is a business related activity.

Check with your accountant on the percentage of the travel expenses and accommodation that becomes business tax deductible, but based on normal practice, it is a percentage of your actual travel costs that you are travelling to, from or remaining in the Suva area.

The virtual office organised tours are normally considered 100% tax deductible.

Visit this web site to see the upcoming tour times and dates.
http://www.businessfreedomlifestyle.com

10 Key Business Outsourcing Ingredients

Appendix 2 - About the Author

About Marisa Wiman

Affectionately known as the 'SME Outsourcing Queen' by her customers.

Marisa developed sound business management skills through exposure to international businesses and corporate compliance formalities from Switzerland through Australia, Fiji, New Zealand, Philippines and the South Pacific regions. Her personal business experience comes from owning and managing nine (9) businesses including over sixty (60) staff in four (4) countries. Working with large multinational companies' right through to a single person business provides the basis for a deep understanding on business management, operational and financial challenges. Marisa is constantly educating herself in business and outsourcing specialties.

Her multi lingual skill provides Marisa with an excellent opportunity to ensure nuance differences and skills match with cultures best suited to the customers.

10 Key Business Outsourcing Ingredients

As this is Marisa's first book, she is looking for your feedback. Visit her web site and share your thoughts.

Marisa's personal invitation to you is for you to call the team and learn what they can do to expand your business or create new opportunities. Visit www.greymouse.com.au or call the virtual team members on 1300 20 60 20 (Australia free call) or +61 (0)7 3118 9594 to expand your horizons.

Thank you.

www.marisawiman.com

Marisa Wiman
Appendix 3 – Tours, Sharing Ideas

Many businesses ask to see how this virtual workforce works first hand. If you wish to understand 'how virtual workforces functions' just visit one of our virtual call centres.

The simplest way is to join our organised tours where you meet the support teams face to face and spend time with them. During the tour business owners learn how freedom and lifestyle choices can be integrated into their businesses.

If you wish to understand behind the scenes workings at a virtual workforce simply arrange a visit with the team at Greymouse. To help business owners, regular tours are conducted through both the Greymouse Fiji and Philippines offices.

The tours purpose is to help business owners understand what is possible and explore new opportunities through personal experience and 'Mastermind Days'.

10 Key Business Outsourcing Ingredients

The simplest way to experience what is possible in your business, is to join our organized tour where you meet the support teams face to face. During the tour, business owners learn how freedom and lifestyle choices can be integrated into their businesses creating massive value for clients and the owner.

Visit www.greymouse.com.au or call the virtual team members on 1300 20 60 20 (Australia free call) or +61 (0)7 3118 9594 to expand your horizons.

To learn about freedom and lifestyle choices in your business, visit our membership site on www.businessfreedomlifestyle.com .

Tour details dates and bookings are available online.

Business
Freedom
Lifestyle

Appendix 4 - Learn More

Business Freedom Lifestyle Ltd has been established for the purpose of sharing business knowledge to the world. Kelvin Davis and Marisa Wiman founded the company to share the lessons that they, and their clients have learned on their business journeys. The journey is more important than the destination, so these lessons come from business owners that transformed their lives.

Additional books written by Kelvin Davis, Marisa Wiman and published by Business Freedom Lifestyle are identified displayed in this section.

These books are designed to help you on your journey sharing ideas, answering the most commonly asked questions. You can purchase copies of the books from these web sites.

www.businessfreedomlifestyle.com
www.lulu.com

E-book versions are also available from the web sites below. www.kindle.com or www.businessfreedomlifestyle.com

To assist you on your personal wealth creation journey I have a complete list of recommended reading located on this link

10 Key Business Outsourcing Ingredients

http://www.businessfreedomlifestyle.com/recommended-reading

Kelvin and Marisa also started Greymouse for the purpose of helping business achieve this goal. As professional outsources and business investors they are constantly looking for new business opportunities.

Speaking events, training and business assistance is available here.

www.businessfreedomlifestyle.com

To order these products simply,

Phone: +61(0) 7 3503 6835

Fax: +61(0) 7 5492 8822 or
Web: www.businessfreedomlifestyle.com
Email: sales@businessfreedomlifestlyle.com

Marisa Wiman

Global Best Sourcing
A tech company must have for maximizing profits and eliminating stress

The technical marketplace has changed dramatically since the year 2000 with changes now measures in months, not years.

To be successful in this industry change is constant and adaptive. Outsourcing is becoming common place, however many businesses still fail to maximize the benefits that come from using this service.

This book is written for the technical entrepreneur, giving expert guidance on the most common challenges and solutions for technical business outsourcing including;

- Partner Selection
- Confidentiality and reliability
- Communication
- Sociability
- Try before you buy

This handbook is for the software, internet, web, hosting and technology companies wanting

10 Key Business Outsourcing Ingredients

to stay ahead of the crowd. This is a 'one flight book' written so you can absorb the critical information within one short plane flight. It is sharp, to the point and without frills. ISBN 978-1-291-77469-6

http://www.lulu.com/shop/kelvin-davis/global-best-sourcing/paperback/product-21593177.html

Available from;

www.lulu.com
www.businessfreedomlifestyle.com

Marisa Wiman
The Secret Road to Wealth
Time to Live your Dreams
by Kelvin Davis

Why do some people effortlessly achieve wealth, while others struggle with no cash left at the end of the week?

The secret road to wealth gives you the roadmap the rich use to create freedom and cash flowing into their pockets every single day. This book will teach you how to;

- Crystalize your dreams
- Discover your inspiration, then leverage it
- Set you income, without working for it
- Recognize the pension trap
- Explode the myth 'time for money'
- Understand what creates your reality
- Master the inner game of wealth
- Reveal the money making machines

Kelvin created a freedom business, one that produces money without the owner's time. Then he replicated this same model in his clients businesses, creating freedom and cash flow for the owners. You walk beside Kelvin and his clients

10 Key Business Outsourcing Ingredients

as they share lessons learnt on every step of their journeys.

Instead of relying on government false promises, create the life you always dreamed of.

Available from;

>   www.lulu.com
>   www.businessfreedomlifestyle.com

Marisa Wiman

Secret Keys to Business Wealth
Create the Life You Want
by Kelvin Davis

The Secret Keys to Business Wealth exposes the reason why some businesses uncap untold wealth while others struggle each day. Understanding the differences between success and failure, then seeing the barriers, gives you unimaginable power.

Kelvin created a freedom business, one that produces money without consuming the owner's time. He then created the same model with his clients. Almost overnight, his owners could travel to exotic countries, or take that well-earned rest.

The secret keys are given to you, explained in simple terms, together with stories of the successful implementation in other industries. Often these small business, range from a single person, (or sometimes without any staff) through to medium size businesses. Imagine learning about this turnkey operation business that just produces income, gives the owner the option of early retirement or allows to expand into other businesses while the team delivers the services needed. Learn how you can implement this in your industry to create new wealth and freedom opportunities.

This book continues from the Secret Road to Wealth teaching about time freedom and cash-flow creating money from business.

http://www.lulu.com/shop/kelvin-davis/secret-keys-to-business-wealth/paperback/product-21624113.html

Appendix 5 – Supporter

The business world is being flattened by economics, technology, demographics and regulations. To win in this flattening world, companies must transform their way of thinking, working, and engagement with partners that help them achieve their goals.

Greymouse Virtual Workforce is an Australian controlled HR provider supplying high quality, time sensitive and cost effective services through its own offshoring facilities based in Suva, Fiji and Legazpi, in the Philippines. The team maximizes the strengths of both countries, plus minimizes outsourcing risks giving clients a massive head start. Customers then realize a freedom in their business that can only be dreamt of.

Greymouse services includes;

- Virtual Receptionists
- Virtual Assistants
- Techies (Marketing, web site and online specialists)
- Information Technology specialists
- Accountancy / Bookkeeping
- Data Entry team

10 Key Business Outsourcing Ingredients

> **Special trial offer by quoting this book's title**
>
> **USA Freecall: 1888-7790643**
>
> **UK Phone: 3308280731**
>
> **Australia toll free: 1300 206020**
>
> **International: +61(0) 7 3118 9594**
>
> **International Fax: +61(0) 7 5492 8822**
> **Web: www.greymouse.com.au**
> **Email: sales@greymouse.com.au**

Marisa Wiman

Notes

10 Key Business Outsourcing Ingredients

Notes

Marisa Wiman

10 Key Business Outsourcing Ingredients

www.ingramcontent.com/pod-product-compliance
Lightning Source LLC
Chambersburg PA
CBHW072229170526
45158CB00002BA/810